IN PRAISE OF MEN
AND OTHER PEOPLE

ANN SANSOM

In Praise of Men and other people

BLOODAXE BOOKS

ISBN: 978 1 85224 633 4

First published 2003 by
Bloodaxe Books Ltd,
Eastburn,
South Park,
Hexham,
Northumberland NE46 1BS.

Reprinted 2014

www.bloodaxebooks.com
For further information about Bloodaxe titles
please visit our website or write to
the above address for a catalogue.

Supported using public funding by
ARTS COUNCIL
ENGLAND

Printed in Great Britain by Bell & Bain Limited, Glasgow, Scotland, on
acid-free paper sourced from mills with FSC chain of custody certification.

Some praise at morning what they blame at night;
But always think the last opinion right.

ALEXANDER POPE
An Essay On Criticism

Acknowledgements

Acknowledgements are due to the editors of the following publications in which some of these poems first appeared: *Art and the Artist, Atlanta Review, Carapace* (South Africa), *Horisont* (Finland/Sweden), *London Magazine, New Blood* (Bloodaxe Books, 1999), *Pennine Platform, Poetry Review, The Rialto, Second Light* and *The Times Literary Supplement.* Some of these poems appeared in the pamphlet *Vehicle* (Slow Dancer, 1999).

I am grateful for an Arts Council Literature Award (1998) and an Author's Foundation award from the Society of Authors (2003).

Contents

Crossing the Nile

A hundred times or more I've crossed just here –
these iron struts that cut the iron Humber
into silver bits, this chunk of train
chunk chunk on slats to lead us in
to long flatlands of always mist and promised rain.

You've been a few years dead, big cousin,
and I haven't missed you much, but here
I always have you in the window seat –
And that, our kid, it's called the River Nile.
I'd thought it might be sea but I was young

and you were streets ahead. Profoundly deaf
and slow at school, you turned out wise and rich,
surprising everybody with a film star wife, a Greek,
who took your every word for gospel
on the strength of your blank face. It seems

you had a way with words, a way of making magic
out of fitments, long settees and space
when crowded three-piece suites were commonplace.
I'm always pleased to hear your thickened voice,
instructive, kind and half believing in the strange.

Breather

(for Michael Laskey)

Having singed my lungs on the steep hill up
I can barely wait to a light a cigarette. You pause,
polite and leisurely and not remotely out of puff
and, while I try to make my feeble lighter work,
point out your morning walk, all this *just look*
made good with early winter mist, an edge of frost.
Up against this endless backdrop I'm in place
but lost. I saw it too. Hugging myself in a big jumper,
I saw from my fuggy room, my sealed window,
the mould-green leaching out of walls, the rotting bark,
sodden fences and your lively dull-red jacket
bounding up the lane. Such energy. I could have
watched forever but sloped off for the camera.
(It printed out as orange, ruby, nothing of the marsh-gas,
nothing of the bleak. I should have known,
with you in it.) Midday, half dead with unaccustomed
quiet and sleep, I hesitate when you suggest a stroll.
My instinct here's to hibernate, but being friends
we stride out to an afternoon of dropping dusk
and threatened snow. It's good for us, I know,
to breathe a bit. We step back for the village bus,
a doggy Volvo and a taxi crammed with kids
you think to wave to. Nothing much assails us
on the slow hill down to Heptonstall. The shop's
not shut for lunch but gone for good. To Let.
We saunter on, put out, and find another, and,
reprieved, I'm reckless with Mars Bars and Rizlas.

Your early walk has left you pleased to be alive.
This village, one night, had the same effect on me.
In love down through the flesh and bone,
I touched his face, relieved to find it warm among all this.
He said, I love these hills, the moors. I felt ashamed
of main line stations, theatres, nightclubs.
Years on you're here and pleased and so am I
we're all of us in different ways alive.

Instructor

This is the best bit; the steep glide into Milnsbridge,
the tight swing under the arch before the home straight,
when I'm behind the wheel, in the last minutes of my hour
and he's there, foot well clear of the brake, mumbling
into his mobile or reaching past me for his medicine.

Twenty-odd years in the Force, he knows about sensors
and patrols, so we sail through the ambers and reds
up to the Cowlersley crossroads. Outside the pub
two constables pause and turn on the pavement to salute us.
A stickler for politeness, he says, 'Wave back. Don't smile.'

I file it under pertinent advice:
never trust another bloke's indicators,
all dogs are unpredictable and ruthless,
know what the real speed limits are,
three ways to recognise an unmarked car.

Mr Montefiore's Pearls

My thirtieth anniversary with Mr Montefiore,
dentist to the stars. *Out at night*, he says.
Not yours, of course. Not yet. And *all this smoke,*
it's dentine powder, not your mouth on fire.
Camp, nervous, bolder than I could ever be,
he peers across the clamp, my half-wit lip,
Four hits will numb you more than just the one.
The fine drill is smoother, quicker, but the thick
more thorough. Priorities. And the mouth
heals faster than any other orifice.
He links me to the door, checks my mascara.
His gloves raise lesions on his wrists.
Pregnant again, you tart? for twenty years,
How come? And now, *I notice you've retired.*
I've learned from him; press down, go harder, longer
than you think you can, the tongue will not obey
the brain, choose powerful men who wince at pain.

Prince
(for Andrew Stibbs)

I study the board like the rules of a dead language
to be memorised, tried on the edge of the tongue
but not applied, not usefully, not this time of night
with the last train shunted out and the porters absent,
cosy, brewing up behind their mirrored door.

Snowed in once, they offered me a drop of whisky
in a mug of orange tea. Not tonight
because rain's a different element;
no camaraderie for those who're wet and late,
victims of their own persistent gullibility.

That time, at least I had a book, Machiavelli.
I read it twice. The station stray snored at my feet.
I got organised and ruthless overnight,
learned how human affairs are governed;
above all else, be wary of benevolent advice.

Tonight it's the Rotherham Star or nothing,
fragile and damp from the bin. Letters, small ads,
garden fork, one tine missing, excellent condition
Massage and Sauna for Business Gents,
Adult Videos, a double spread of Lonely Hearts.

The realpolitik: *fortune is changeable
like a woman* or an April timetable
*but a man of goodwill is obstinate
and usefully predictable*, a snooty dog
that comes to heel. Good boy At least I know your name.

Gossip

This winter you have the sea on three sides
and so you sleep and wake and sleep again.
Each morning you wake
into a bowl of lamp-lit quiet. Astonished
because you'd learned the lie of that

the year you almost drowned –
a little accident in France brought on
by too much drink and too much nakedness,
in weeks of tight unbroken heat.
Strange, you thought, to surface

in that river and go down and down again
and face up to the same black tangled trees,
the moon, the same small friends
out of reach; and you, drawn under to the weir,
already giving up but taking note:

it's easier than you thought, easier
than striking out, evading a broad grip
more powerful and more tender
than the letting-go of sleep. Who'd have guessed
all that racket as your lungs deflate,

bubbled voices reassembled wrong
into a mouthful of your children,
riverweed, the why and what of who you love,
and then the last time down a chunk of something
you might spew out later on the bank.

But now you wake, delighted to turn on the radio,
make tea, compose a letter carefully to a friend
surrounded by the selfsame sea,
who has other plans this grim new year
inside his island solitude, the makings

of a sturdier boat, the residue at least
of what the Jesuits offer up as argument.
My love as always, you type out, *my love*.
The sea rants on. You potter on the beach,
take the letter to an empty box.

He answers with a sharp account about his goats
and yes, of course, these January tides...
Nonetheless, the postman – him – rows out
with homemade wine and candles, and his cello
wrapped in a blanket against the salt,

to share the gossip hereabouts, which,
as he reminds you, is God's word.

Rowing

It's proper here to look one way and row
another, to balance water and go back
across a lake I'll look at later,
my oars in service like a camera
to catch and lift what I'm too busy for

and let it fall, a spool and then
a wallet fat with dated saturated snaps
I'll gather up one of those quiet times
I never get. At least not quiet like this,
this morning on a shallow lake

designed for boating amateurs.
No other trade, no punters here
to smile to see us run aground, capsize,
to drag one of us out. Just lilies
flat as well-aimed plates, the surface

settled like a long dispute. I dip
and dredge. Draw back and breathe
against my arms, my quailing guts.
Lean a moment. Learn what matters;
him in the stern, that book propped on his knees.

Providence

Rain shields the valley
until the hills come back greener, darker
and winter switches off. Sogged air runs lighter,
birdsong sharpens on the thunder of the weir.
Someone tinker tinkers fails
then launches out on the piano, the phone
rings pauses rings and quietens, answered.

You're at ease before the good news comes,
the great good news, the cavalry despatched
and sighted, land ahoy. The letter due tomorrow
comes today. You find relief in the beginning
of the end, the change, and set your clock an hour ahead
to meet the nights already drawing out. You claim
the windfall with your needs already met. He thinks
he loves you and you think he's coming back.

How to Survive at Sea

It's tricky so make sure you have the book to hand.

Seven chapters
Solar Stills
The Power of the Human Will
Sharks
It's unreliable
but try the section on *Making a Spear-gun*

pump in the evening rest in the day
big fish are suckers for barnacles
crying drains salt off the vital organs believe
your brother will come back for you keep a log
and always remember a wave is not water
but something that happens to water

learn to enjoy the haddock's eye, its juice   it's juice
shouting dries the throat   keep busy fashion things
harpoons out of forks or chains of paper-clips

sellotape keeps varnished desks afloat
flares take twenty seconds
boats pass   don't count   *Flares*

don't count on being rescued by the rescuers
small fish fight back   rip holes in rafts   pure spite
ignore sharks   miles of glittering salt   read
when you get the chance   light your last flares

then turn your back   get hauled up   *Ropes*

kiss the book   drop it over the side
concoct another: *Survivors and Small Fish:*
the most dangerous creatures on earth
Don't have your kids aboard   *Don't*

All you need

After all, it was the walls I missed;
white as a hospital, the ceiling an ironed sheet,
the coving clean as icing. I remember every inch.

And the windows up for the heat, summer after summer
all that year. I thought it might be something else far out
too much – the violet carpet or the *nothing you can say*

with somebody to lift the needle when it clicked.
But it slid October, December, then chock,
a caught matchbox, then bitch bitch bitch.

To Judo

Orlando, the big brown horse I mounted by mistake in France
or the ski lift where I lost the use of my legs through vertigo
but walked away or sometimes driving now when I fly
through a sudden junction, hair's breadth and weightless
as a pinch of salt. I remember you.

You were my gentle art, my chance to celebrate what I was good at –
submission and a form of fruitful dislocation.
With you I'd step out on the mat and offer everything I was
to a polite implacable opponent . Mine, the leaden face
of the found-out monk, nothing of my own to lose,

and his a blur beyond the belt, the higher grade
I ought to want. I only saw the balanced bulk of white
above, below the black. I bowed to that. And you,
you were the cold in the thumb I barely recognised
but prompted, knew to close it, firm, on his ironed jacket.

And you were the backward step I took. There is honour
you said, in every wise retreat. So run away with confidence.
At first I never had the nerve. I fought. A cornered rat,
the savage spearing out to find itself pinned down.
From you I learned to hesitate, give in, fall hard

and right, come up as if I didn't mind. Judokas play,
nobody wins. You just walk on, back off, head down
like someone working out a set of moves then move
and do it blind. Again. Until you're fit to drop. Until
it's in your hands, your feet. From you I learned

to make a habit out of recklessness and luck,
to shuffle on the edge, to recognise the give
before the break, the slam designed to jolt the heart
and spine. I learned to leave the leaving train
and close my hand on his lapel.

In Praise of Men

Generally speaking, they know such a lot,
and tell you some, if they feel like talking.

So, it bothers me, that print – *The Beguiling
of Merlin* – how it's hanging, not quite straight

between the windows in the bedroom.
Lovely but unjustified, I sometimes think,

to pick a wizard's brain and leave him snared,
betrayed, condemned, petard, and by his own book

too. All that wisdom and turned to wood
by a wicked woman. It bothers me, generally.

Ad majorem

Mostly they're spoiled priests, mainly Jesuits,
Dei gloriam or *semper fidelis* they close the letters –

rich accounts of *vis inertiae* and the madwomen
who've befriended, screwed and hampered them.

But you, my dear, are the exception
and so, nil desperandum, ergo, ego, I am.

Milk

(for E.A. Markham)

It was here at dawn, this thin stretch of shoreline,
this window space; a drenched battalion of mounted men,
steady hooves in slack slow shingle, him at the heart of them.
She slept on, her face fat with peace, her boats beached

tied up, home and burned. He might have said, might say,
no safety, least of all from me but he's struck dumb, equipped
for eating on the hoof, an odd disdain for salty goat's milk tea.
Trained and maimed. She'll tell him one day, 'You've gone numb.

Old mare's milk rots the brain.' And then in bed, the matter of
        the goats,
the sheep, the geldings and the men who'll make him what he is,
who'll teach him how to strand the stallion's tail for guitar strings.
Coltsfoot for coughs, for hussar's piles.

The archer shoots and turns and sighs and runs, the reins embedded
in his hands. Attila Genghis Jesus Christ. He weighed eight pounds
six ounces and his calloused foot pushed hard against the stirrup
of her index and her thumb. His palm was stars and triangles.
His father's father's eyes looked up to hers amazed.

Anchorage

Spying is waiting for life to provide
a moment of choice between the vagaries

of an isolated place and the patches of peace
in dungeon fog. You can't hunch yourself

against the fog but you can put your faith
in the drink that stills your hand, the gift

for inappropriate, unseemly dress. Politeness.
Remember to smile in the right place. Beam.

Report: Both men retired early to their kingdoms.
One slept. One talked all night. One rose

at eight to pound the cliff-edge in his oilskins,
dragging his elderly yellow dog,

one doubled his pillow, adjusted his specs
and settled to his book. Spying is quelling

mindless fear. The ocean here is green.
You're often left alone to plan the spring

of vicious honey-traps, the presentation
of developed evidence. You haunt and wait,

employ the rigid tradecraft you once learned
to preen yourself against. Belief, they said.

Prepare for one disaster and expect another.
Circle possibility. Rehearse assassin's ecstacy

but bring no harm. Take note: Iscariot
the patron of us all, hailed a jovial taxi home,

remembered to tip well but kept his silence
like the deepest love hugged in his bony chest.

You will leave the island – so much of life is will –
and begin alone again. You will

once you've made the mangy labrador drop dead
and the king's book fall astonished off his bed.

Her Women 1463-1489

And now to business;
one kneels to the linen chest, raises the lid
for swaddling, one fills a shallow dish,
one spreads towels, one dabbles water with her fingertips.

Two conspire. Two console her, offer her the child.
But what concerns her here is what's outside
the curtained door, what comes after.
Nothing more, they tell her, *nothing worse*.

One wipes the hefty wooden secateurs
one drags a sodden mop, two bundle sheets
and rags, one tends the stove. One leaves
and comes back with the priest.

'Sounds of grief...'

Sounds of grief are unbecoming in a household such as ours
SAPPHO

Three lifelong friends, a tideless sea,
Metaxa, Ouzo, mornings in the nineties.
We've learned to say 'Hello, how are you?'
Étsi k'étsi, he answers, offering his wrists, *So So*.
He's got us weighed up but his taverna's cheap,
two minutes from the path down to the beach.

The only women in Anaxos, we swim when we like;
in the sunrise, in the dark and go back barefoot
wrapped in salty sheets we won't have to wash.
Salt leavens everything, shakes everything to bits
but leaves an afternoon of monastery steps
translated to Our Lady of the Sweetest Kiss,

a fist of honey cake donated by a headscarfed woman
on her knees. We were never thieves but want
to pacify a nursing cat who's at our heels.
We light four yellow candles, leave them burning
for the people we love best, for shame, for choice:
to rob a sweet-toothed priest or starve an animal.

What friends are for

What friends are for, to stop you going out too far;
and counting on each other, we're already miles astray.
It's mild for March. We're here to say goodbye –
soon you'll be in Brittany for good, she's packed
for Adelaide. And so, a little drunk, reluctant
to go back, we're heading for the sea almost in step.

The drained bay's like smoked glass but soft
and each foot's lighter than the last. Nearer,
the long white crooked wall is only foam,
the dim black roar is tons of turning water, nothing more.
Horizon light, a rim of guesswork now, will disappear.

We're on a darkened balcony to overlook, say, Greece,
that first night with the tree rats and the mix of thyme
and cooling brick and goat. Or France, bleak dawn,
a sheet of mercury we broke and breasted through,
somewhere else like this, right on the edge of earth and safe.

Gemini

More than half a lifetime of intensive yoga, veganism,
daily meditation for the promotion of a positive aura and

in the interests of balance

an occasional excess of wine and men and nicotine.
The stress that you let gather out of hand

then grasp   then loose

has left you with the sheen of adverts, balms and pricey creams
that let you down in certain lights and will not ease the thinner skin

about the neck, the mouth, the eyes.

Mischief, insomnia and candleflame beget composure.
You have the face you've earned,worked day and night for:

a woman on her way home

disciplined and hurt out of a health farm or an unwise night.
Toned up relaxed alert a measure of sang-froid

a kind of paradise regained.

And so, and yet, the driver scorns your Senior Pass.
Full fare he says. A woman of your age. As if. Well, yes.

For Belle in Brittany

The year's begun badly, grown worse;
death, love, uncertainty, inquest.
Enriched and hurt, you've bought a house,
a stretch of water, a small boat, a ticket.

Friendship's behind you now. It's time
to lock my door out of this world,
return the key you painted white
so I could always find it in the dark.

When you arrive and rooms shuffle
bare boards, strange furniture, bound crates
and you wander the windows, stairs
in and out of vacancy, you'll miss me.

When the light fails, you'll rest. Morning
you'll uncurl, refreshed, complete as a cat.
Wherever you are, what you always were,
your own woman, your own home.

Catering

We enter quickly, settle for a table
near the door, no fuss. We hang our coats
on chairbacks, stow our bags and wait.
If there's a menu we scan it, guess what's really on
and decide on that, prepared for disappointment.
We tap ash into a matchbox or a pocket
sooner than run anyone about.

We take note of the office party,
gauge the suits, the white wines and sodas,
the steins of lagers; know who'll be first
to handle the waitress, who'll blush
when she leans across and whispers.
We recognise who'll send the chicken back,
who'll leave a tip, who's likely to throw up.

And the fraudster with his cards and *cheers*,
his mislaid cheque-book, the anxious drunk
fingering the wine list, the querulous
who make up allergics and want to know
what's in the cock-a-leekie exactly,
the loner who dithers for company, and the couple,
sullen or so fat with love they've got no appetite.

And while we wait, we rearrange the mats,
wipe the salt and pepper pots on napkins
(refolding them to butterfly or mitre).
We keep our feet out of the aisle, our elbows
in. We never click our fingers. When he comes
we're civil to the waiter, knowing him
for a thoroughgoing bastard of a nose-picker.

Battalions of us, working undercover,
our youths misspent in such establishments,
who keep a penchant for flat shoes, for vegetarians
who frown and choose but never cut up rough.
We give our orders with the gentleness
of ordinary paying customers
or Michelins or Public Health Inspectors.

Cats

Generations behind him:
thatchers, slaters, installers of aerials,
solitary, aloof, barely domesticated creatures
who stalked out of kitchens, bristling
and retired upwards
to curse and spit in their proper element.

On the tiles, two or three storeys up
they'd crouch, a menace to pigeons,
or sprawl astride the ridge, supremely indifferent
to decades of mothers wives sisters
who lift their humble disadvantaged faces
and call from far down fields and back-yards.

She knew she could add her voice to theirs,
plead him down with a meal, an apology,
and he might descend, or settle himself
to lever a wedge of moss from a gutter,
consider a warped slate, finger the mortar
on a chimney stack. In his own good time.

Instead she did what the women always did
in the end. It was in their blood.
She poured herself a drink, lit the candles,
dragged an easy chair close to the fire,
opened the book and began to sing
The Incantation to Bring Fierce Rain.

At Edie's

It was always the racing: York Newbury Epsom
and Edie rearing out of the sofa
with her no teeth and soft bare legs
bawling some laggard on
Goodgodalmighty, man. I've ten bob on this'n.

Four girls roughly my age (*all fillies,
sign of a happy marriage*), a dad away at work
and Grandad Len, *always got the monk on,* him.
She'd set him off on his circuit in his mac
Armson's to lay the bets, Zanelli's shop, the beer off,

round to Armson's for the winnings. I felt blessed,
learning gambling for profit and what it bought –
buns from Hills's and a crate of stout
and Len allowed to rest, his cap off,
with Edie holding forth on *picking a good un,*

till my mother raked me out.
You've the brains for it, Edie'd say. *I know.
Winners. You and that Marilyn Monroe.* My mother
complained to the priest and made it illicit,
though he liked a bet himself and quizzed me after.

Edie says Lester's worth a fiver to win, I told him.
She's been down to the gallops and –
(Go on, go on, he said) – he's his arse to the air
and it bodes well in the Leger.
By my friends, he said, shall ye know me. Yes father.

And your mother has your interests at heart,
she thinks you need a dose of salts but I suspect
appendicitis. In future, you'll avoid
the Edies of this world. Now, a few novenas,
one or two First Fridays, let's set her mind at rest.

After that, Edie bought a poodle and the first car
in our street and their Elaine got pregnant
and Len dropped dead in Armson's
collecting, they said,
thousands.

33

St Augustine's House

Star of the Day all afternoon for bursting head down through the line,
the remains of the relay team gone mad on the far side of the track.
Well done, St Augustines. Team effort, team spirit. Not mine, then.
Not even when I come coasting in off the sprint, eyes shut, hands up.

Even the man who lands every week with a suitcase full of bagpipes –
ignore him, girls – pauses in his slow adjustments. Even Sister Sebastian
wants to smile. It's fifty merit points to St Augustine's House, my
      house.
It might redeem the end of term disgrace. It never does. Lost cause,
      won race.

So this – *you will not run in corridors, you will not ever raise your voice* –
is my own not quite controlled explosion, my private celebration
of the mastery of the thigh and heart and inflamed throat. No need
      for style
or grace or piety when you're invisible, so quick you don't exist as flesh,

until you sink into the grass with something vast and small, intangible
      and grasped
and loaned and kept. Well done. A minute's pleasure calling back
      the breath
well spent in service to a form of indolence, a minute's peace, a
      coming to,
before – not yet – the Honour Shield to St Augustine's hopeless house.

A Portrait of the Duke

Eight weeks break and we've worked every day;
you on your portrait of the Duke of Wellington,
scraping down, starting again, but cheerful.
You've got the chin, the narrowing to pique
dead on. This time next week you'll have an inkling
of the socket, the brow, a hairline. Maybe not.
It's eight-thirty and we're a queue of two, loitering
outside the museum. You've heard he's in the café
in full uniform and you want a scan at the profile.
I'm hiding my sketches of Bob Dylan, wanting
not to fight about ephemera, though I'm tempted
on the step under the wire-mesh Epstein to confess

I've memorised a three page rant you'd shudder at,
I've seen the best minds – You what ? You've seen nothing –
...of my generation. Thirty-odd years on, I marvel
at that memory; to hold a mouthful of jism and moloch
before I'd even looked them up. Mostly we agreed;
Keats'd be alive today if he'd met one of us,
Byron'd harden into glad fidelity, Wilde brazen it out.
But shoulder to shoulder in the drawing class, I flagged,
reviving under praise I never had the stamina to earn.
And you, censured, sharpened up, started again.
Every portrait a campaign, a set of stratagies, a tussle
you might win. For me, a pose; a jawline shaded

till it sagged, a lazy lid, contracted pupil, then
a lucky highlight on a hand that couldn't grip.

Enlightenment

It seems you've reached a conclusion,
put your affairs in order, burnt everything
and taken to ringing your friends
with apposite unyielding quotations.
Mine came secondhand, nothing of your own
but it's still true, I think, that it takes two
to cut you to the quick: One friend to speak,
another friend to bring word back.

It's true I keep the faith when it's convenient,
and true I broke the buddha; Woolworth's bakelite,
fragile, slippery as a conker. It cost us seven and six.
But I held on to the good bits, his words
to comfort those who're left. It changes. It changes.
I remember that. And some tradition, just enough
to seal the senses, thumb them shut
with liberal quantities of oil, a little salt.

I know to turn you over with a proper kiss.
Tell her it's Judas gets to write the biography.
Last words, old love. You really think
because it's deathbed stuff it's holy writ?
It's shite. He never wrote a word, too busy
with the loot, the rope. Why not remind me
that the wheel turns and we have to bank on that
or this – a sharp backhander taken at the wrist

and clasped can be a palm held open, offered
to the dark. Duality, enlightenment.
This is the sound of one warm hand.
Take it and close it as you like.

Night Ferry – August 1950

They'd had trouble getting there –
a problem with her boarding pass –
but he'd talked them through
and up into the night boat.

Almost midnight, a cold dockside
and him six foot in his good overcoat,
taking someone aside for a word.
I'll have a word, he'd say.

And never mind how uniformed and surly,
they'd always bend and let him in or out.
His tilted trilby and her crippling heels,
the fur lined gloves, the generous New Look.

They liked themselves, they loved their only child
and saw themselves as blessed, reprieved
from poverty and tribes. It's kids, she said,
too many kids, that keep us poor.

That breakfast in Portrush; good Irish tea,
unrationed bacon, heavy bread. She said
the waitress envied her her big fine man,
her little son, and thought her married very young.

She said Belfast was bleak and left her numb.
And then, one night they crossed a border in the dark
and silent dwarfs in waders carried her, a feather's weight,
across a moonlit field and dropped her in a boat

and then strode back, braced up for him.
She said they sagged bow-legged, groaned,
next night when she came back; the pounds
of contraband she'd looped up in her skirt...

We'd egg her on to tell the tale again;
the cold dockside, the chancy field,
and them, still free of us, still blessed;
the time they liked each other best.

Before the Wake

Shutting the door on the priest, And thank you, Father,
the title coming out so easy, a wonder
I don't genuflect as well. In the front room,
no one now but you, still sitting by the bed,
trying his hand against your own. Still warm,
he has the greater span. 'I can't believe he's gone'.
Neither can I and unable to reach out,
to touch for comfort, I say 'Trust him.
He'll come rolling in at closing time
with the trilby on back to front, upsetting everybody.'

I'm clumsy with the sheet, shifting you away,
trying to tuck him in. Futile.
I know he'll open that hard mouth:
Pull yourself together, lad. Look to your sister,
her with the hands like shovels, much like my own.

Where you go from

You share a room with your brother
because it's warmer and he can stop you
wandering in your sleep because he's bigger.
Odd then, how fifty years on,
for all your efforts to escape that bed
and stumble on the stairs and maybe

break your silly neck, odd
how many times you'll come to,
rattling at the knob, still half asleep
determined to get in that room –
the diamond lino, wool and paraffin –
the one you'll always have to cross
before you start to dream.

Ghost, Sleeping

Old man Rose, home off nights, sat hours
dozing on the step, content, patient, happy to be out
all weathers, sooner than wake his pretty wife.
According to legend, anyone up in our house
in the small hours might see him; a tiny man, grey
with pit muck, slumped benign against our door.
My dad said, 'Many a morning, when I'm on early days,
I draw the curtains and look out. Dead or not,
I'd fetch him in. A nice chap, old man Rose.'
Our gentle ghost, kind to dad when he was just the boy
next door, and it seems a meanness to enquire further,
and yet I'm woman enough now to wonder why
she slept when others crept those stairs half-dead
to fettle grates, scrub backs. A nice man waiting
for a beauty who'd not stir from sleep for him.
Not for her the fire made-up, the kettle to the bath,
the bacon pan, the welcome home unhurt.
At a time when other back-doors shut on snecks,
and ghosts roamed distant castles, why
was ours always bolted top and bottom, locked?

Playing Patience with Uncle Jack

My certain source, you draw yourself up
to address the slates, a chimney pot, a passing bird
Am I – a long exasperated sigh – *an information bureau?*

Well, no. And we walk on in silence.
Before you ask: Bureaucracy:
a hierarchy and some connection with a desk,
a kind of cloth. What am I on about?

I understand you're mad
because this afternoon I placed the red queen
on your stagnant jack as if I knew the rules, as if
I'd no respect, as if we'd decades of experience between us,

rather than your shaky hand, a smeared glass, as if I weren't
the timid niece the Sisters hammer into dull obedience.
Me and you, we play for ha'pennies, for keeps. You can't do
with half measures, watered drinks. I want steady answers.

Uncle Jack, I love you best when you are wise and wordy
and triumphant. I'm at your hip when you're the scourge
of doorstep tradesmen, window cleaners, carol singers,
my cold enlightened faithful catechiser of Jehovah's Witnesses.

At cards, I always win because I'm terrified
you might upturn the table for my daftness. *Girl*, you'd say.
A man who might have sired sons. I cave in, memorise
each card as if I'd never know another rigid man

who'd marry once and so forever and amen. *Patricia.*
Look it up. But she ran off with orange hair, a hatred
for the horses and the drink. Where is she now?
Search me. Somewhere. I place a tidy winning hand.

A strumpet always ends up in the right.
At dominoes, most lenient of games, I learned
to clench my toes and taste what tension really means.
Until in thirty, forty years, another man can say

'I'm pleased we're only friends, there's nothing,
no frisson (*a hairdresser?*) between us.' I'm faint
with disappointment and relief, holding four flat kings.
He plays a three, a deuce and then takes leave

to strip his pale green sweat-marked shirt, his vest. I fold
and I blame you. At least I would if I were twenty-one
or fifty-two. I'd say I never learned to play an honest game
or show a card without you on the other side, alert.

To you who never dealt to lose but often lost,
I'm offering what you'd scorn. To you who taught me
how to love and doubt: Familiarity Ineptitude Apologia
Place Your Lousy Rotten Cards Girl
in Some Frigging Sort of Order John O'Hara.

2 Para

In the hall reaching down his overcoat,
I get the scent of it; dark damp wool
heavy as the wardrobe we hid in once,
the whole house gone mad
and one of us peeing in fright
on the heaped shoes, a hat-box of photos.

Tonight, he's looking out, judging the sleet,
and I could lip-sync it – *Brecon, that time.*
They stripped us bollock-naked, had us sprinting
on the ice. Special Training. You don't know you're born.
Lines I've memorised, a play I've seen alone
and failed to grasp *Aldershot Aden Belfast.*

He swings the coat, easy, drawing me in the draught,
his fingers hooked in the lapels. Stepping back
he settles the biased cut of what is after all
a skirt, feeds leather buttons, conkers on plaited thread,
offers a padded spine, square-shaved neck, my profile.
For me he'll smile his perfect teeth, unbend, exhume

familiar Bushmills Old Spice Golden Virginia. Nothing to fear.
I put my hand to his shoulder, turn him from the mirror.

Winchester Slide Action

And if I told you again about the night
the Head went for me with a blow-torch
and how I hid in the lavatory, crouched over Yeats
or Tennyson, memorising and how it was the making of me,
you'd be patient and generous and cuddle in
and not believe a word. And in truth, you'd be wrong.
It sustained me, helped me perfect the accent, this one
that lulls you, warms you into kindness, distance.

And the scar you finger, here, this finger. Xavier,
adept with a ruler edge. Yes. You know him do you?
Yes. Just hear me out and then we will. We'll dance
the early hours forever of Brown Sugar, Green Onions,
Fontella Bass. Rescue me and we'll dance the night
the floor came up to meet us in a place like this:
my beret blown to bits, the badge a sheaf of needles
in my mouth, my boots clear as glass for seconds.

A miracle, I am, a gift, a sweet good afternoon in Derry,
not this that shuffles sideways, hard, afraid to press it in
against not you, you someone somewhere else. Utopia,
nowhere. Sweetheart, I'll see you right. You smile, mime deaf.
I talk a lot of shite. You hesitate. Lip-read. And sobering,
I wonder what you want. You mouth it, measured
and sincere, *thought you'd never ask.* And laugh.
The bar's a brilliant choice of greenish nuts, wet mats,

square jugs. He draws mine quick, one handed, back turned
to the optic, then bobs relieved under the counter,
to delve a bottle out for you. Family, no charge, he says.
He's pleased you're here and sober. This floor is safe. It is.
I've checked. A nightclub changing hands each week,
same clown, new dickey bow, his boys rigged out in black,
your cousins on the door. I'm posh, a welcome guest
in Yorkshire, a headcase in the barracks with my quotes,
my box of books. The Falls a different matter.

Here, we're talking sex and history. We kiss.
And I'd put folding money you could name me
every Irish Martyr in a quiz. But now you move a little space
and me, I have a lovely face, a voice that echoes
from a mirrored place, a corridor, a master, Sophocles,
his wig aslant, his gown askew, and there is no old age
for anger only you. You're hot and dying on your feet.
Your brother has a blue tattoo I've kissed in fear. He stalks us,
smiling, terrified. Lean in and listen, love.

I'll drop a rope before too long. We're trained. We move in step.
You're very very very soft.

Taking Sanctuary

This is the summer, endless as good summers are,
and coming down to one exhausted evening, here,
contained, the dark blue trees and sand and cooling sea.
And if you choose to rest you'll rest, or else
you'll wade, you'll plough a thick strand longways
through the shallow end, no lasting wake, and you'll decide.
By August you'll decide. Nothing hinges on your choice.
You choose a walking meditation – stay or leave – turning
when the skyline gives at Portland Prison, turning back.

Sometimes the dark breaks in the orange canvas
and you want your dad. You want him bigger
than the searchlights and the booms commanding swimmers
to turn back or drown. Remission's in the scales
but not for you, somebody else, not you, your jeans wet
to the knee, your shoes safe in your narrow tent –
illicit, innocent and private in a private wood at six o'clock.

Who'd mind. You pay your way, take on unlikely work
and work but not for long; the circus or the Slipper Baths
or minding sheep or weeding gravel paths for nuns
through afternoons of stunning heat. It's summer
and you're seventeen. He'll be a long time dead.
Tonight you'll wade a bit before you sleep and slide
content into a hell of guarded gates. It's paradise, he says.
First streak of light, you pack, hitch up through Dorset, out.

Finding the fox

It was the end of December, if I remember right
and bitter as it always was: the market longways to the river:
ironed-up jerseys, cobbled boots, a five bob rummage.

I was warm enough. I had the order in my purse,
your number, and there the bus I ought to catch
and there I saw it swinging from a distance.

At first a brassy ruffled fleece, and then, close up,
each separate pelt was salt and rust, a sweet
bloodorange honey flame, the flame you find in things that set,

a leisurely and latent heat. Five pounds. The bus moved off.
Decision. And I wore it long enough. That day I ran
and told you (when they'd let me in, thank god, that screw,

the soft one, shouting *Come on, red*), 'You would have stopped
for that. You would.' And yes, you might. A too long coat,
silk lined, and every skin a featherweight, a whim. You smiled.

The impulse in us both to hesitate, then panic far too late.
Years after, we were sitting up, the house gone quiet,
my kids asleep, the coat long buried near the tip,

and you recounting great escapes – all farcical, all failed
for all your cunning and your sweat – until
we reached the dogs, the sirens and the dogs;

you and Casey cornered in a greenhouse in a park,
trying to prise the cuffs off with a rake, your wrist
a mess and worth it, almost, for a moment,

to take off your hand or his. A nice kid, Casey.
Last I'd heard he'd joined Jehovah's Witnesses,
set up a stall in Leeds; Security Devices, Doorbells.

Doing well. 'Happy Ending, then,' you said,
as if we'd learned something.

Pedigree

Five years since you went south on a whim
and bad advice, lugging your small credit,
your real class, leaving me your books, your posters,
a nest of thriving debts. And I thought you'd stepped out
of your childhood, kicked it aside, an ill-fitting
shabby skirt – but when did you own either one,
you with your lanky denim legs – when did you ever
toe the family line on little girls and women.

An athlete from the off in a team of talkers,
drinkers, shiftless wankers. And the men no better,
predators with their weakness for a fight,
the sweet little number, easy in and out,
no sweat, no comebacks. Those nights you couldn't move
for bottles: who'd put his hands up, who could do
a five stretch on his head, who might get a good result
and walk, or break in Durham or in Armley.

Their father's uncle's brother's business.
You didn't know your place: the child among us
to take notes, to sit in years of waiting rooms, grow
expert on the wording of a warrant, the etiquette
of open visits, letters, sudden home-leaves.
How come, you asked, *We're all so smart
and we're not rich?* From me, they might have laughed,
an auntie with her heart in the right place

a bit too much upstairs, maybe, but never lippy
in mixed company. *You what?* I could have dropped
when you repeated it, *How come.*
Your mother and my mother and your sisters
waded in – it's kids that keep us poor.
Would you shut up? Well, no. Eighteen, you want
your say, and say it in a now-hollow room:
an acid tongue of argument to stake against

the sawn-off and the boot, the charm, the wit,
the prick that balances the steady pint
and pays the rent. You weigh your first year Literature
against the deconstructed legendary.
Not impressed. O Kath. Alter your face. For me.
Just smile. It's far too early for the fight
that's breaking out. You don't wrong-foot a pack
that's shaping up to scent a grass, and worse,

a female who's not one of us. Keep quiet
or show your ignorance of when the mouth
comes open, when it shuts. My dear gobshite,
I just sat tight and hoped you'd make it out. You might.
Outflanked, outnumbered but rangy,
fast on your feet, you gained a little ground,
a measure of respect. You slipped that leather jacket on
and went. They blamed your schooling for the sudden quiet

in what had been the makings of a damn good do —
your brother's — meant to compensate for years
of sloppings out, corrupted visits, failed appeals.
And so in time you're implicated
in grievances, ruined nights in overheated
brassy hp deep-piled maisonettes. You came back
with a clinking bag. If I remember right
we sang, we drank, we danced a bit. I flirted

with the ten-pint-sober uncles as I always did.
You, I'm sure I kissed goodnight, distant, mindful
of that morning *wrong, the wrong wrong woman;*
we woke up; me in my boots and gloves
and overcoat, and you foulmouthed and naked,
still drunk enough to speak, *O fuck. If only you were
someone else.* At least you got the grammar right.
And now I worry. Not a proper family trait.

Aren't we by nature careless, brave
and murderous liars? Don't we plead only
in mitigation, in defence? In this sort of gamble,
I'd bank it all on instinct, speed, a set of broken links.
Another thing — I dream you're hurt, desperate
for your own, tempted to call. Don't you know fine
they'd come mobhanded, keen to haul you in.
Forget the phone, recall the Christmas Eve

your sister bit a rival's finger to the bone –
how you dived to catch the ring and, hesitating, failed
to pocket it. Think on. Years of splitting the spoils
and you were here, studying the view
from this window, your back turned, nursing
a half-broken heart. If I considered you at all,
you were luminous and white, frail, graceful,
it was the wiry fine stringbeading of your spine.

So I answered, the glass to my mouth,
and the vague anxiety of an appointment missed,
and the ranked battalions of my own troubles
– no excuse – *if you're in doubt it means you have to run.*
They wonder how you manage to survive, exiled,
way off your own patch. *No word. Not hide nor hair.*
The little bitch. And I wonder what you've taken
from their wisdom. *Keep your head down*

when you can't keep your nose clean, keep your friend close,
your enemy closer, blood's always thicker.
Trust no bugger. The dogma of the loser.
A little is bred in the bone but not everything
we have is tribal. We come full circle, we return.
It's not the same as coming home. Your postcards filter in
from Highgate, Camden Town, handed on
from old addresses in my other names –

I'm fit. I'm getting by. Hope you miss me. I'll write soon.
And then the thief's farewell, *Be lucky. All my love, Kathleen.*

Crooks

in Crookes of all places; as far removed as you could move
from this red-light dive, dealers jostling punters outside
Caesar's Sauna, go tooled up to the chip shop
nobody in their right mind postcode. We like it.

But then this street's the curve on the figures,
hemmed in as it is by St Jude's and the vicarage.
You're asking for it, if you ask me, cosying into a district
noted for its rectitude, its niceness.

I've found it's often safer in the thick of thieves,
sharing guttering with robbers. Good fences
make good neighbours, especially if
they're your uncles, brothers, nephews. Family,

I'm all for it; Love and Hate tattooed on knuckles.
You know where you stand in Paradise Road, Belle Vue.
Remember that estate named after poets:
Wordsworth for the problem families, De Quincey

for smack-heads. Place names are more of a request
than a label, a sign of what's lacking. Look at Hawes.
So to move up to Crookes, and then go all astounded
when you turn the key on nothing left, everything

binbagged and changing hands
before you'd hardly caught the bus...
I'd come home if I were you.
It's where the heart is.

Nancy

That woman reared a tribe of pagans, my mother said,
and your father among them, knowing no better.
Until he married, of course, and shaking off his wicked mother
mended his ways and took to milk and Mass like water.
But we liked her, admired the corrugated hair,
the pearl-drop earrings, her fingernails a set of tiny pillar-boxes,
the sauntering high-heeled slippers where others trudged
in turbaned curlers, grey men's socks. And the language,
her neat painted mouth pulled down, regretful, prim,

And so I had to tell him straight, she'd say. *I told him
he could arseholes, for me.* Her final word on everything
from parsons down to royalty. Too bold by half, braving
the pit-top to tell the manager what he could do with his five bob,
refusing to stand for the Anthem in the Legion and barred *sine die*
for her favourite verb. *They can arseholes,* she'd shouted,
parasites, battening on the poor. As if the poor
were someone else, not here, not her with her debts
and her old scandals. (One Christmas Eve, she'd set off

for the butcher's and turned up next day with the goose,
legless, a disgrace. *I met some pals,* she told us,
You know how it is.) And how is it with thirteen kids
and weeks of strikes and a man who laughed and cried,
that pleased to see you back. How do you keep that fine hand fine;
the ring to the pawn, and in between – Monday to pay-day
it's cold water, black-lead, soda, and a sacking apron to wipe it on.
We knew nothing beyond your jokes, the birthdays, weddings,

parties lasting a week, you leading congas in the street,
your spindle legs tireless in the glassy shoes through your seventies,
your eighties. And then your daughters in their best colours,
clashing perfumes, the front room spiky with wreaths,
your quiet sons weeding out the lilies. *I'll not have lilies
in my house,* you'd said. *They're for the dead.
Any bugger dares to send me lilies. You know.
You can tell them what to do.*

Linthwaite

The moon is not a nice man
IAN McMILLAN

More of this bitter Pennine rain, icy
and unclean, but today I'm refreshed by it.
Walking home from swimming, scoured hands
in my pockets, I'm almost at ease,
composed enough of water to notice
and admire the vicious brambles, sturdy reeds,
the pocked greasy face of the river.

Mostly I'm here to contemplate the worst
of possibility, to measure paranoia
against certainty or to exercise
a mongrel fear and run its legs off
on the sliding gravel. But it was here
my youngest son asked the impossible
and I said yes and thought but god forbid.

And he went on ahead, satisfied
that if the moon were real after all,
a man in a scarf and specs and gloves,
he could look in our house and see us.
This morning, a rigid self-regard
dissolves in memory and gratitude
and childish trust. It turns to puddles

on the slimy tow-path, turns to pleasure
in a raddled bridge that shifts
and then completes its circle underwater.
Here, between the shallows
and the vacant pasture, I'm free to speak
out loud, to stumble unobserved,
among the vast indifferences of nature.

Diver

You pick your way, bow-footed, wavering,
but this isn't genuine hesitation;
it's a style, a manner of moving
you've rehearsed in your head to perfection.

The shallows of your spine, the muscles in your thighs
are toned and fluid. Your body mounts the steps,
brings you firmly to the board,
your face stuporous with trust.

Beneath you, the surface is coarse but unbroken,
a roughly ironed linen. The rising smell
is damp sheets off a line, controlled decay
that means well, like ammonia, like sea.

There's nothing to fear. The future
will close over you without hunger,
burble calming nonsense, and place
a fine green glass between your mouth

and the air that you once struggled for.
Your terror, compressed to a slim grey stone,
will skim briefly on the surface, then disperse,
forgotten, foolish as a solemn promise.

Nothing pursues you, wants you more
than this, the element that you can't bear.
It is faith and fear rather than love
that bring you to the edge, year after year.

Here you're a guest and free to leave, of course.
But turn your back again and, this time,
you risk a downpour that won't stop, a river
that insinuates itself under your door,

a cold lake that opens in the darkness
between your bed and waking life. For politeness,
for your own good health, raise your hands,
flex your knees, bend your stiff neck,

and dive.

What we spent...

What we spent, we had. What we had, we have.
What we lost, we leave.

Epitaph for his wife and himself,
by the Duke of Devon, 12th Century

Let the dead be an example to us.
We still believe, still see them
pouring coffee, raising a mug we bought
in Whitby and broke between two houses,
packed though it was in a whole Examiner
because it was one of a pair, the other green
if you remember, though you don't need to,
having it here, an extra in the photo.

And that breakfast bar
we meant to rip out, first thing, first day,
but it came in, for reaching the ceiling,
for ironing, for heaping bills and cat hair on.
The shelf at your shoulder; two struggling ivies,
a coffee pot I could still lay my hands on, if.
A dim blue dish, the half rim of a clock,
one fingertip at three; wedding gifts we kept.

Here I seem to have you, him
in an eight by six, and any second now
the shutter drops and he looks up and smiles
or speaks, his grip loose on the mug, his mouth,
his eyes alive with love that keeps renewing
in response to blood and time, a flash.
Let the dead be an example to us; the words,
the presents and the flesh they leave behind.

Vostok

Once Antarctica was warm and forested.
The lake was bright with boats, swimmers,
the shore rich in good hotels, casinos.
Families gathered for their winter festival –
stems of lanthorns, remnants of leather leggings,
thousands of families.

Today, three miles down, the lake
prepares to present a history preserved
by the rigorous purity of polar ice.
A life so slow, almost undetectable,
like the deep pointless hibernation
of microbes in bricks baked for pyramids
or in the stomachs of frozen mammoths
dead ten thousand winters.

A million years cut off from the sun
that goes on shining on nothing new,
water schooled in patience and potential
is seeping through. The clearest water
anywhere on earth. And how you read it,
that invested water, measures you.

Opening the Vodka

Which brings me back to how at that sort of juncture
like most lapsed Catholics I'm party to a spectacular
self-mania – the one where the host slides in, late,
darlings, an eel! and proceeds to bash its brains out
slime on steel above the built-in leopard skin. A cocktail bar
where I attempt and fail again to open the vodka.

Give it here honey, his finger's on the neck, *Let me.*
You've seen Withnail? My eldest is six foot three.
He taped it, sat night after night committing it
to *I assure you, officer, I've only had a few ales*
bawled from the bath he lolled in, a hard blue faceful
of Body Shop's 'Just Scrape Your Skin Off Then'. *Bring me*

your finest wines! I lend him Hendrix, he bows
to my experience, just like his father. Both of them are saving
for a Fender. But I don't talk too much about my kids
to youths like this who offer me a reference,
your hair's a plague of rats. High praise. I'll celebrate
once I've got this sodding top off. *Let me.*

I could have been a bartender. Ignore him now
and wrestle with the icy thing I want by my own effort
opened. Wince when he goes on *I could have bartended.*
O you semi-literate stud, I like your leather balaclava,
almost as much as I admire your anxious partner
in the clingfilm acrylic and bumpy suspenders –

until she asks and have you any family?
because at this late hour I'm not talking babies,
not to a child much like my own, every last one of them,
who never cried or slept, and she, with him, perhaps,
is keeping in her house and under wraps *almost*
a mirror image of her mother as the room turns under her

and she's propped up by the host, *allow me,*
who opens a Fred Fellini's Freezer Shop carrier
which she tries – tricky in those gloves, the sudden sweat –
to close round her face, neatly to bring back the curried prawns.
And it's here that I step out, to ring a taxi, grasp the common sense
of adolescence and, in a moment of grace, refuse one for the road

from him in the tank-top and half-moon glasses.
But there is no taxi. And so he pours and by now
she'll be upstairs with her poshest knickers to her face,
why do women do that wet expensive sticky lace, cold now,
but warm enough when she took them off –
and there are sound hormonal reasons to just check:

a sudden access of fertility, a scent you'll remember –
Instinct, I tell my daughter. *I knew before the cigarette*
and forget that morning, almost drowned in my own bath,
the keynotes of a cheap and fruity perfume
in my ears, the green silk skirt voluminous
about my mouth, my former husband's hands

locked on my throat. Are you in love? *Hands up*
who's in love? – a question unforgivable at parties
but she'll ask it later, here among the licked plates
and glasses, and Balaclava Boy won't answer.
Walking home, I worry about her, that girl
(you'll feel much better if you bring it up)
and about the host, still hobbled in those handcuffs.

Vehicle

Tomorrow, you'll be told this car is lethal.
Even the mechanic will back off from it;
the wishbone almost snapped, the engine bouncing
loose at every turn, a miracle it's not dropped out
on the road to Langsett Barn.

But tonight, you reach for the green-lit dash,
turn up the radio for a violin and flutes
and the baby a week from birth obliges us,
raising her knees, pedalling against my ribs.
Warm at last, we ease out of scarves

and take the long way to see where it leads.
The new city rewinds on the dark, returns us
to miles of slick steep road, snow swilled off fields,
dark villages we coast through, in no hurry.
In the back, our eldest nurses an axe,

hoping for difficult logs. Either side of him
the others jostle, elbow for space.
Firstborn is never a fortunate position.
They envy him the axe, the carring,
his silence. He endures them.

They'll learn. Eventually, they'll learn
responsibility. The weight of being trusted
with a weapon. Hard work. Decision.
Up front, we give up on the map,
let the headlights bring us out, at last.

Hagg Hill, Bolderstone, a dozy owl,
until a grind of gears and, dropping down,
we make the turn for Langsett woods.

*　　*　　*

We slide on mulch and frozen stone,
duck under branches, filing down to where
the reservoir shifts smoke inside the boundary wall,
not water at all though the trees sound like a sea
of needles and branches, breaking on remnants
of leaves and grubby sky. The children work,
their gloves slimy with sodden bark
and I, unbalanced and idle, wedge myself
in a system of knuckled roots and wait.
Here, I'm all agreement, gifted with children

and a minute's peace. I want for nothing,
no miracles aside from this. Home,
we'll tip the spoils out on the hearth,
reprieve this one with the snout and mane,
a beaten horse, and burn without compassion

the spiny rest, wanting warmth. We talk
on the road back, while the car labours and protests
then relaxes on the downslopes, at speed.
The kids sleep. Behind the wipers, secure
and warm, we're rocked almost into sleep.

Felix 12

It comes post-marked the week before.
I'm writing this against a bumpy coach
travelling to the birth plan place
– you've evidently hesitated here,
and come back firmer – *of William the Conqueror.*

You think I'd like to hear about *the tapestry,*
the tons of photos – gallons it turns out
of molten channel, a mass of heaving grey.
My love, it's you I really want to see,
the foxy hair, the sidelong smile,

but you're the camera-man and haven't learned
that cold prints out like dull. Years after,
you'll contrive to drive me mental
with your scribbled notes, your obsessional
Fender cradled rampant on your knee,

can we for once before we all go mad
just eat in peace. Can we? Go on then.
Pick my brains for Muddy Waters, Hendrix,
Clapton, Richards. Go on, provoke me into
that one time with Morrison. But trust me son,

I know I shout but then again
aren't I the one who dreamed the day before
you'd come back safe and harass me to death
with all the whys and wherefores of a shell?
Felix, you tedious insomniac,

you brilliant pest, I keep your sharp-edged
oddly-given gift among the debris
of my desk; a token of the birth plan place,
seen before I saw it, a chunky whirl
of blue-veined mother-of-pearl.

This is the life

an hour between trains,
a solid bacon sandwich,
a mug of milky tea, a *Guardian*
spread out at the middle page;

a one-day Travelmaster,
a set of half redundant keys,
a fistful of loose copper.
And to rummage in my pockets

but leisurely, a small anxiety
for ten or twenty ps. *Phone us.*
I have this empty buffet
for thirty, forty minutes,

time enough to roll another,
and get out the hardback
like a housebrick
I cart around in hope. A refill.

I never saw the mural,
Icebergs in Spring, before today
or how the optics have been angled
to measure more or less. In any case

I'll be on my feet soon,
down the platform in a blast of rain, to call
because I can. This is the life
in which I never fell in love.

This steamy idleness is all my own,
a life in which my children were not born.

Album

In these gummed pages – the far reaches of a park –
you gesture at me (the camera), furious
or just bored, agree to perch on the rim
of a dried out fountain. You raise thin shoulders,
the shelved expensive haircut that was cool then,
splay the trainers that cost months
of double paper rounds. Click. Your brother
bowls past, shuttered to a blur of red-striped shirt
and cheek and blondness, years younger, framed
in your indignant hands. A good summer.
Your nature tempered by a new guitar,
an old despair made calmer by your sister.
On your way somewhere, held here.

Felix 21

When Balby Road is endless before you after you
and you're trudging   trapped in your navy jacket
stooped   under what for what's the point

may you find that you've straightened your back
lowered your shoulders lifted your face   surprised
to discover yourself   almost arrived   beyond

the Sorting Office and the Corner Pin and then again
the subway   lost briefly   but up in to the sun
and into here my love in no time   keep walking

Naming Names

One for the world, one for the family
and one for your own sweet self. But I,

with more names to my name than Soft Harry,
have been too greedy, easy come

forget them, spoiled for choice and ruined
by a string of saints, distant patrons

with their virtuous untrue histories.
Begin with the chosen few dripped in

another set slapped on at seven,
then the ones for fancy, nicked, arising

out of each other, or made up in panic,
for a form, on a whim, the pseudonym

that roams and thrives and takes on
over time flesh of its own. The world.

Water Feature

A green brass H tap out of his shed,
a central heating pump that sprayed the street
at first, higher than the house. But then,
a couple of nuts off a boiler he was saving,
and you've a water feature
to sit out summer nights by.

You weren't in his class when it came
to ordering from *Screwfix Monthly*
but you've an eye for salvage,
what might work. You light the lanterns
he welded out of bits of bike,
kindle sticks in the oven he head-standed in a skip for

and contemplate gaps in the greenhouse
he didn't after all dismantle to take with him.
It's then you notice, propped against the bin,
that quarter of the landing mirror,
jagged but big enough to set behind your fountain
and double everything. Fabulous.

And now, this morning, a blue tit after crumbs
catches sight of what there is in there.
He hesitates mid-scout, hops up to look.
You're entertained. He cocks his head. It's charming,
though nothing comes of it however hard
he preens and pecks and hops and pecks. Hours.

You phone your sister. He's getting mad.
Advised, you hang a shirt to make him disappear.
He perseveres. Tries to force round the back.
His tiny heart. A minor tragedy
is brewing here. You think he thinks she's
just as desperate, and he won't give up.

You say out loud to an empty room
the stamina of love. But then again,
it's late, you recognise a hopeless cause.
Hard luck. You drop the blind
who's crying, who gives a flying.
Which is when he rings. You hesitate.

Clematis

A fist of knotted shoots bobs in on a sly draught
then out into the fog; a gift I might acknowledge
even yet, forgiveness I almost accept
on your behalf and mine. I placed the borrowed ladder
coaxed you up and armed you with my little knowledge,
my passion for the radical. Occasion of your error
with the secateurs; in my defence, I had my wrists
and elbows bound in loops of overgrowth, a weight
of shining snails against my face, a grim desire
to free myself from what I thought was dead. We knew
at once, between us we'd gone wrong, hacked off
the succulent and left the spiny twig. Now this.

Slugs and Snails

(for Mad Dog Richards)

I've chosen the perfect murder; cleaner
than what comes home from a trek in the dark
to the lay-by, the sewer. Neater and wiser

and no shoes to burn, no spattered mac,
no bloodshot tears to fake, O no, against
some slow Columbo taking note.

It's more the staircase and the firm heel to
the trusting nape. Simple. Unlock, step out
and sling a handful of sky blue, retreat.

By morning, a platoon of vacant shells ooze
their last on the grate. But I can't rest. Some days
I'm good at guilt. Their precious life,

their weakness for my hops. I hook them out
and think how best to work –
decide to hoik them into Andrew's yard:

he won't mind, he gives them beer. Next time
I'll take a hammer and unhouse the loathsome
creeping crawling sods. It's politic, honester.

Spring

The tail end of March and a morning for creeping out of fog,
squinting at signs for Slackbottom, Thistlebottom, Airfield Keep Out.

A morning for thanking God for flasks and radio horoscopes:
Lucky number: Four thousand and four. Lucky bag: Gladstone.

And The News. The world is still out there, not going under,
however many icebergs meander down to Doncaster.

There are radiators and lifts and painted-up transoms
over cities that thrive beyond these furlongs. Acres

of full-length mirrors in canalside flats, a man shaving,
and look, a fox studying the fountains in the Peace Gardens.

In the Bering Straits for instance,

fifteen foot rollers heave for centuries under ice-packs; milling,
    subsiding, falling
flaccid under glass they never trouble. Never so much as a lick of
    salt against the surface
they could melt. Then unprovoked one rears, breaks out to sever
    tow-ropes, to swallow
a ship, a crew inches from heroic rescue. The thwarted yellow
    helicopters. Sudden peace.

Malicious, you might say, if you saw it on a film or in the thick,
    embarrassed to death
in a scarlet suit, having been coaxed into a basket, then slurped
    back, a living harvest.
Sly, bullying, mindless. But think how nicely it linked your arm
    one afternoon
in a cool sea off the coast of Wales. A kindly, firm induction, in
    private, into grace

and humiliation. No one to notice, no marksman to aim a line and
    fail. It came
in its own time, flexing its chewed grey muscle, drawing in the
    last of the sun,
sparkling a slurry of salt and blasted shell and easing into sponge
    the leadweight
of your self. And later, how easily it freed you, shamed you with
    indifference, softness.

Delivered back with the gift of small cuts and your life condensed
    to this, *you might*
have come and laid with me, unhurt, learned what it is to teem with
    given life, to wait,
to breathe in peace, to want, to make the whole world flirt.

Lady's Bridge

The river comes through the city,
clear black even in summer but tonight,
late January, it's cracked at the weir
on burst red stars, bus windows. You could die
of cold, this lead frost could weight
your lungs, pile stones in your pockets.

But tonight, he crosses the bridge.
Sometimes he's gone adrift, wandering
into step with a similar jacket, a woman
towing a small boy and shopping bags.
Tonight, his gloves swinging, he can move
and be still, present and future, harmless.

Sometimes those early dark afternoons
the river runs a glinting ink over prints
of railings, streetlights, faces, his.
But tonight under his numb shoes,
his vacant coat, his cap sparked with sleet,
nothing. One in front, then the other.
He'll be home before you know it.

Idling

A last peaceful cigarette. The bottles rinsed,
lined up in the crate, the cat browsing the step
casual, alert. One day all this will be yours;
restrained grass, absent weeds, flown greenfly,
these rigid loopy rags of clematis, disciplined, snail free.

One morning you'll stand here stunned. And satisfied
you draw on the stub, reward yourself for a job well done.
You might celebrate, get a haircut, a massage,
finish something. The cat curves in, worn out, yawning.
In the morning all this will be the paradise you potter in,

toeing heaps of charred flock, striped mattress ticking,
the gold-threaded ostrich egg of your melted phone.
Go in now. Deadlock the door, hook the chain, go right up
to the attic, turn in, sleep tight, sleep well. Work
is arranging itself, getting done to spare you the trouble;

wires undress under floorboards, a carpet smoulders,
your wardrobe warms towards its contents, an old blind
hesitates, gives in, subsides in languid plastic drops.

Since

He's taken over up there.
Days lounging in the stump of the house
under the hanging decay of the roof.
Nights. A thud when he drops off
what's left of the sill, then pads through
his suite of caves. Hours in the filth, ruffling
the pounds of Victorian soot that came in
with the ceilings, old breaths floating down
into cupboards, mirrors, beds the fire missed.
We eat it, smear our foreheads with it.

I want it sucked out, some gigantic vacuum to arrive.
He slinks about in black elbow length gloves,
his fur staring with old plaster, hideousness,
the remants of disaster on like a sumptuous mink.
He strolls down for breakfast, sits up to the table,
his face thinner, eyes ravenous. They warned us,
the Red Cross who come to these things.
A pair of evangelists who whispered to us for hours
under dripping floorboards, banisters scored
by hoses dragging glass from major incidents.

Any spiritual problems, let us know. *Respiratory*,
they must have said but my hearing was fixed
on the flying sparks, the small crack crack crack
of him at the biscuit bowl. Revelling, he was.
And every day since, more like a Persian Blue,
superior, proud creatures but clean. Not like this
obscenity, this flue brush. I'd have laughed once.
But a week before Christmas, sleet slanting through
exploded glass, barely a working light or socket
and half the artisans of Yorkshire stomping big boots

up the remains of my carpet. The more liberties he takes,
the more I'm reminded of some pagan deity, the insane
red raving mouth of a settee, thick orange claws circling
the centre of a rug, and the sound that divides the animal
that was from this, a sound that took me curious

and casual from the landing to the back stairs, quite at ease,
mistress of my own house, owner of a harmless pet
who padded at my heels. Hearing before sight or scent
coils of wiring giving up the ghost to let it loose,
something like a kitten's idle, silky sneeze.

The world is everything

Where I come from the language is water,
the essential beat of a line is tidal,
a sweep of blood to the heart
before the slow boom of a mother's voice
and her outer voice that breaks
to let others in, for manners.
The rhythm is sleep and turn in sleep
and rock awake and rest.
There is tedium without idleness.

Where I come from the ocean is pink
and framed and warm; belly breast face
an unclaimed inheritance as we roll
and flex in that roundness, lithe and slick,
trouble undreamed before us,
our only distress a thumb lost to the lips
a surge of spite in a tangled cord.

Where I come from we love our dark life;
we won't give it up, though we all leave.
There's no question of betrayal.
We develop a selective personal amnesia,
and deny the maps and diagrams we half believe
as if we might in fantasy have been there,
nothing more. Our hearts steady, our eyes clear
and our tongues begin to dry and falter.

Eyam

Here's a nosegay; a pocketful of sage
and bramble, a gill of dragon water,
oil of elder. It's potent as hard winters
sent to curb a plague and sharp as ice-packs
in a pillowcase against a fever.

But would he listen, when he'd heard
the delf in limestone rocks crying to his Lord
for wisdom. Lord. And failing that, they said,
grant us in your goodness, in your mercy
and forgiveness, a firm undoing of the past:

to see the carrier's horse dropped in the ruts,
the bolt of cloth delivered pure and dry.
A simple prayer; let us not know what we now know
and learn again each morning with each child, each loss.
Thrown rocks.

But he believed in greater plagues; eternal death
born of depravity, infection warmed in human flesh,
sin's gorgeous flea-bites; greed and lust. We ask
for common health. We ask like him, too late,
a miracle and just this once.

Feeling Lucky

Off your own manor, as it were, going West –
a different tribe altogether – so you're looking for portents,
tokens, and before long the magpie shows up,
pointed, defiantly solitary however long you hold your breath.
But you know where you are with that, what to say.

Then before it's said, there's the wolf, almost a wolf, and you ease
your brakes on, stop. Let him lope in his own good time, let him
turn his peppered head, his yellow eyes to you and blink and go.

It picks up after that, real life, houses, pubs, pavements,
and a runner catching his breath at a view of fields
like first jigsaws, dull but possible. Then barns. And reservoirs.
See the good in things. It's not yours but it's not forever.
You'll be going home later. Pull yourself together. Windfarms.

And the radio; Beatles, Christmas 67, yapping like hounds
because they can and the Stones jangling out of jail, *we love you.*
Nothing terrible is coming down. In a wolf's mouth, *in bocca a lupo.*

Blessing the House

I love this house as much as trouble does
and so, in opposition to the fire
the flood the broken glass the blood
the tireless tiresome lumbering in the yard
the wolf with keys the mindless cunning
in the cellars and the green roof space
I might I must concoct a form of words
to drive it out and keep it out. Enough.
Begin with that. And end, perhaps.